Contents

Tables

Origins of the Second Nuclear Crisis

"Time is not on your side."[1] North Korean vice minister Kim Gye-gwan spoke these words in January 2004 to Charles Pritchard, the former US special envoy for negotiations to the Democratic People's Republic of Korea (DPRK). These words are more true now than in the past. During the Cold War, the Korean peninsula was a sideshow beside the main act of US-USSR tension. Of course, South Korea was important to the United States, but only as a player in the overall US policy of containment. South Korea added no intrinsic value to US security. Likewise, the DPRK was only important to the Soviet Union as a bastion of communism in a world of capitalism. Neither the United States nor the Soviet Union was going to risk a nuclear exchange over the Korean peninsula. The situation was bearable if not stable. The demise of the Soviet Union changed this comfortable reality.

The fall of the Soviet Union and the collapse of communism in Eastern Europe had a profound effect on the DPRK.[2] With the Soviet Union no longer a controlling and generous patron and Kim Il Sung stunned by the whirlwind of unwanted change throughout the communist world, the DPRK invigorated its self-reliant military policy. Feeling increasingly isolated, the DPRK intensified its quest for nuclear weapons.

In 1993, the DPRK refused to allow the International Atomic Energy Agency (IAEA) to inspect two nuclear sites to confirm if the country had been separating plutonium for nuclear weapons. The situation quickly heated up.[3] The DPRK threatened to engulf Seoul in a sea of fire while the United States prepared for military action amid calls for air strikes against DPRK nuclear facilities from respected strategists such as Brent Scowcroft.[4] Fortunately, war was averted, with intense high level diplomacy resulting in the 1994 Agreed Framework.[5] It is important to understand that the situation could have easily resulted in conflict prior to the signing of the Agreed Framework. As Korean expert Young Whan Kihl has said, "Threatening rhetoric and gestures reached such a point that the 1994 Korean crisis might, indeed, have gotten out of hand and plunged the Korean Peninsula into the tragedy of another hot war."[6]

The event that precipitated the previously quoted words of the DPRK vice minister was the revelation in 2002 that the DPRK had begun a uranium enrichment program in violation of the 1994 Agreed Framework. The Bush administration responded to this violation by stopping delivery of all US obligations (heavy oil and light water reactor technology/equipment) under the framework. The DPRK responded by unsealing its Yongbyon nuclear reactor, reprocessing spent fuel, and extracting plutonium twice—obtaining enough plutonium for eight nuclear weapons.[7] The second nuclear crisis and the race against time had begun.

The purpose of this paper is to explore how the United States should engage the DPRK on the nuclear issue. This paper will outline two reasons why the current multilateral talks should be abandoned in favor of a bilateral US-DPRK approach. The first reason is that the Six Party Talks produce results too slowly for the situation due to its organization. Second, the talks rely too much on the questionable influence of China. Next, having made the argument for bilateral talks, the paper will outline the two critical steps the United States must take to achieve denuclearization of the DPRK. First, the United States must completely understand the DPRK position and second, the United States must repair and strengthen its alliance with the Republic of Korea (ROK).

After learning of the DPRK's resumption of nuclear activity banned by the Agreed Framework, the Bush administration ceased bilateral contact with the DPRK and settled on a multilateral approach to the crisis. The resulting Six Party Talks, of which the United States, Russia, South Korea, Japan, China, and the DPRK are members, began in April 2003. What little progress was made in these talks was shattered by the October 2006 DPRK nuclear weapons test. The Six Party Talks continued following the test and produced an agreement in 2007. In return for heavy fuel oil, the DPRK agreed to shutdown its nuclear facilities once again and promised to make a declaration of all its nuclear activities.

However, problems still remain. A former director of the Los Alamos National Laboratory who visited the Yongbyon site three times, admitted the DPRK had "retained a hedge to be able to restart the facilities if the [2007 Six Party] agreement falls through."[8] He estimated it would take only six to twelve months to restart all facilities. Also, the DPRK has not disclosed nuclear activity at any site other than Yongbyon despite US conclusions that the weaponization facilities are located elsewhere.[9] Furthermore, discrepancies and omissions in the DPRK nuclear activity declaration have yet to be resolved. The lack of information regarding the DPRK's enriched uranium program and a discrepancy in the amount of reprocessed plutonium are the most significant gaps. Finally, in the spring of 2008, the North Korean Ministry of Foreign Affairs admitted that the DPRK had slowed the discharge of spent nuclear fuel from the Yongbyon reactor, bringing into question the DPRK's commitment to the Six Party agreement.[10]

Based on this information, it is difficult to assume that this is the end of the crisis. The DPRK has a long history of challenging the United States with bad behavior to achieve tangible benefits, such as economic aid.[11] The DPRK has mastered coercive tactics, such as threats, ultimatums, crisis escalation, and brinkmanship.[12] The United States will need continued engagement on this issue until the final, complete, and verified resolution of the nuclear problem. However, such engagement cannot take the shape of military force.

The costs of a military solution to the problem are extremely high and will involve casualties the US conscience cannot afford. In 1994, the Commander of Combined Forces

Command Korea, General Gary Luck, estimated 80,000 to 100,000 American deaths in a new Korean war and a total cost to the United States of one trillion dollars.[13] Of note, these numbers assume a conventionally armed DPRK and do not include South Korean civilian and military casualties or the total economic costs to the region. In a different assessment, General Luck estimated total casualties, both civilian and military, at one million and total economic damage in the region at one trillion dollars.[14] Furthermore, any preemptive attack against the Yongbyon facility, in an attempt to limit costs or casualties, would cause the DPRK to launch an attack south. Referencing the Israeli airstrike against an Iraqi nuclear facility in 1981, General Luck stated, "If we pull an Osirak, they will be coming south."[15]

Problems with the Six Party Talks

With the costs of a military solution intolerable and with the understanding that the situation is far from resolved, continued United States diplomatic engagement on the nuclear issue is needed. The question now becomes what should this diplomatic engagement look like? My assessment is that the United States must decide on a bilateral approach, engaging the DPRK directly. There are two major reasons why the current multilateral approach, in the form of the Six Party Talks, is not the best avenue for the progress that is needed.

First, the current Six Party Talks are too slow to achieve results. Time is a major consideration in this matter. The Six Party Talks began in August 2003. Four years later, in 2007, the Six Party Talks yielded an agreement. Unfortunately, it took less time (three years) for the DPRK to restart its Yongbyon facility in 2003, reprocess fuel, and test a nuclear weapon in 2006. The primary reason for the slow progress is that the Six Party Talks are too inclusive.

Granted, the multilateralism of the current arrangement can be viewed as an advantage. First, it denies the DPRK what it truly desires the most, a one-on-one between the United States and the DPRK. The DPRK's long held position has been that the nuclear issue must be resolved directly between the United States and the DPRK.[16] Next, the forum increases the regional pressure that can be brought to bear on the DPRK to verifiably dismantle its nuclear program. Finally, the multilateralism overcomes the objections of United States domestic factions that dismissed the Clinton administration's Agreed Framework as "fundamentally flawed because it excluded South Korea."[17] However, these benefits are nullified by the disadvantages of the Six Party Talks.

While the strength of the Six Party Talks may be its regional inclusiveness, it is also a significant weakness in that it increases the complexity of the negotiations. Each participant has a different reason for wanting to be part of the Six Party Talks. One example involves Japan. Of utmost national importance to Japan and its people is not the nuclear issue but rather the successful resolution of the abduction issue.

In the 1970s and 1980s, reports surfaced, and were subsequently confirmed, that the DPRK had kidnapped Japanese civilians in order to train North Korean spies in Japanese culture and language. In spite of the fact that the DPRK fired a missile over the land mass of Japan in 1998, resolution of the abduction issue looms larger for Japan than the nuclear issue. When Japanese Prime Minister Junichiro Koizumi flew to Pyongyang in 2002, the purpose of the visit was not to address the DPRK nuclear program or its ballistic missiles. Instead, Koizumi asked Kim Jong-Il to "arrange a meeting for us with the surviving abductees. And I would like you to make an outright apology. In addition, I want you to provide information about the deceased abductees."[18] While the security threat posed by the DPRK is obviously of concern to Japanese policymakers, the abduction issue ranks higher. However, introducing such a highly charged but limited national problem into the Six Party Talks is not beneficial since it does not further the movement to denuclearization of the DPRK.

Beyond the example of Japan, Charles Pritchard, the former US special envoy to the DPRK, offers what he believes to be the priority of each country in the Six Party Talks:[19]

United States – Eliminate North Korea's nuclear weapons program

South Korea – Prevent any increase of tension on the peninsula

China – Preserve peace and stability in the region

Japan – Maintain access to North Korea to pursue the abduction issue

Russia – Be seen as a Pacific player

North Korea – Manage or limit potential damage from the United States

Pritchard concludes that "[k]eeping track of the national interests and strategic goals that each player has in the six-party process can be a bit confusing."[20] Moreover, we can see from this list that while each player is drawn to the process by the same issue, each comes to the table for a different reason. Therefore, when the United States proposes sanctions as a coercive tool against the DPRK, US partners in the Six Party Talks, especially South Korea and China, oppose them because sanctions conflict with their individual policy goals. Cooperation and consensus become more difficult as the number of players increases. In assessing the Six Party Talks, Young Whan Kihl stated that the US decision "to involve other actors in the nuclear talks, under the umbrella of the six-party Beijing talks, may make the situation more complex and complicated than if it had confronted North Korea face to face."[21] This misalignment of each country's policy goals makes the Six Party Talks slow to produce the needed results on the DPRK nuclear program.

The second reason the Six Party Talks are not the best opportunity for future progress is that they rely too much on the influence of China on the DPRK. Until the late 1990s, when China began to rethink and reshape its role in the international community, China had always demonstrated a consistent pattern of loyalty to the DPRK. As patron to the DPRK, China had intervened in the Korean War, replaced lost economic subsidies upon the fall of the Soviet Union, and stymied any efforts in the United Nations to apply economic sanctions or condemnation on its client. During the first nuclear crisis in the early 1990s, China refused to expend any political capital in pursuit of a regional solution to the dire situation despite requests from both Seoul and Tokyo.[22] China was an obstacle to a solution rather than an avenue to an agreement. It was influential with Pyongyang, but refused to use its influence to pressure the DPRK to stop its nuclear weapons development.

However, the situation began to change in the late 1990s when China heralded a new security concept in which it embraced the role of a responsible great power. The premise of this concept was enshrined in China's 2002 Defense White Paper: "To enhance mutual trust through dialogue, to promote common security through cooperation, and to cultivate a new security concept featuring mutual trust, mutual benefit, equality and cooperation, [*sic*] have become the requirements of the new era."[23]

Appropriate to its shifting role in world affairs, China enticed the DPRK to trilateral talks with the United States in 2003 with promises of greater economic aid.[24] Later, China maneuvered the DPRK into accepting the Six Party format, despite DPRK claims to "never participate in any kind of multilateral talks."[25] With China now willing to leverage its special relationship with the DPRK through economic aid and political pressure, the obvious conclusion is that China is the key to a "diplomatic settlement of North Korea's differences with the world."[26] But events have cast doubt on this assertion.

In July 2006, China urged Pyongyang not to proceed with its announced ballistic missile tests, but to no avail. At that time, China took the unprecedented steps of temporarily terminating crude oil deliveries to the DPRK and supporting the United Nations resolution condemning the missile tests.[27] Three months later, an unfazed DPRK exploded a nuclear weapon despite urgent pleas from Beijing to show restraint.[28] These events bring into question the influence that China has over the DPRK and China's ability to bring the nuclear issue to a conclusion that is ultimately satisfactory to the United States. This reflects negatively on the prospects of the Six Party Talks.

Another problem exists with the idea of relying on China to influence the DPRK in a multilateral environment. China's use of leverage in the Six Party Talks may be self-defeating. By applying pressure on the DPRK, China may be giving up what little influence it has by appearing to the DPRK to be too agreeable with the United States and its position on the nuclear issue. "Some Chinese commentators fear that as a result of China's increasing tilt towards the U.S., China's leverage over Pyongyang has decreased."[29] Pyongyang certainly understands the nature of its relationship with China and is necessarily "wary of Beijing's international influence, its ability to collaborate with the United States and South Korea, its willingness to foster traditional friendship, and its credibility in fulfilling its commitments to the DPRK in case of crisis."[30] The conclusion is that China's influence over the DPRK will become less potent as China continues to apply its leverage.

Finally, it cannot be ruled out that China is hoping for an outcome that is in direct conflict with US policy goals. Some Chinese academics have argued that a nuclear DPRK is in China's interest. Shen Dingli of Fudan University claims that "China may see some degree of [nuclear] proliferation as in its interest as leverage over the U.S. in its pursuit of concessions over Taiwan."[31] Presumably, by nurturing the DPRK nuclear program to a demonstrable level, China could trade this program for a pledge from the United States not to intervene in Chinese actions against Taiwan. This is a dangerous proposition for China and assumes that China could control DPRK nuclear actions after enabling the capability. However unlikely, this does demonstrate a danger of relying on Chinese influence over the DPRK to settle the nuclear issue.

Bilateral talks will remove these two critical problems. A bilateral agenda can exclude distracting regional issues to speed up progress as well as reduce the reliance on China's questionable influence with the DPRK. Getting the other four members (China, South Korea, Japan, and Russia) of the Six Party Talks to agree to a bilateral approach between the United States and the DPRK may not be difficult as each member, with the exception of Russia, is unhappy with the current progress.[32] In fact, South Korea, China, and Japan are working on their own diplomatic initiatives outside the Six Party Talks.[33] Having reviewed the merits and rationale for abandoning the Six Party Talks in favor of bilateral negotiations between the United States and the DPRK, it is necessary to consider what steps the United States should take to solve the nuclear issue in a bilateral forum.

Moving to Bilateral Talks

Unfortunately, simply deciding on a bilateral course is not enough to ensure success. The United States still needs a comprehensive strategy, beyond the format, to guide its moves in the bilateral arena. The remaining portions of this paper will outline the major strategy themes that should guide the efforts of the United States government as it negotiates with the DPRK over the nuclear issue. First, the United States needs to understand the DPRK position and, more importantly, the rationale behind its agenda. As Hans Park wrote in his book, *North Korea: Ideology, Politics, Economy*, "Without understanding Pyongyang's intentions, any effort at negotiated settlement will be futile."[34]

To understand the DPRK's intentions, the United States must grasp the most fundamental aspect of North Korean ideology, namely Juche. It roughly translates as "self-reliance". Juche has forever been the central focus of the DPRK's national identity. More importantly, it has evolved into a militant nationalism that "invokes hostility against foreign hegemonism and promotes supremacy of the Korean heritage and its people."[35] Juche heavily shapes the actions and attitudes of the DPRK leadership. But Juche cannot be fulfilled if the sovereignty of the state is not preserved. Therefore, as a prerequisite of Juche, the security of the nation must be the first priority of DPRK political and military leaders. And for these leaders, security has always been achieved through military strength.

It is very easy to characterize the actions and intentions of the DPRK as crazy. Unfortunately, this characterization reflects an inability or unwillingness to think critically about what motivates the DPRK regime. Rather than being unpredictable, irrational, or crazy, perhaps "North Korea has taken a course that is perfectly congruent with the desire to maximize its own comprehensive national interest."[36] In other words, the DPRK subscribes to the realist school of national security thought. So it should come as no surprise that the DPRK is concerned about the ultimate self-interest, the security and preservation of the state. For all the bluster of DPRK statements, such concerns have often been articulated. The DPRK response to President Bush's "axis of evil" speech in 2002 was that it was clear the United States intended "to violate the sovereignty of the DPRK, openly interfere in its internal affairs and stifle it by force."[37] One consistent DPRK demand of the United States has always been the signing of a peace treaty with a nonaggression clause.[38] In lieu of such an event, DPRK security demands a strong military and the possession of nuclear weapons.

While the DPRK has mainly viewed security in military terms, it may now realize that the economic costs of maintaining a large conventional military are undercutting the security that force was meant to provide.[39] As seen in Table 1, the DPRK military strategy dictates that the South Korean technological advantages in military equipment must be countered by numerical superiority. The DPRK maintains a strong conventional military that is the fifth largest in the world.

Table 1. North and South Korean Military Personnel, 2003-2004

	North Korea	South Korea
Total Armed Forces	1,082,000	686,000
Ground Forces	950,000	588,000

Beyond personnel, the DPRK possesses numerical superiority in almost every category of military equipment, including tanks, armored personnel carriers, artillery, rocket launchers, missiles, naval vessels, combat aircraft, and armed helicopters.[40] Quantity is needed to overcome the South Korean advantage in quality. But this numerical superiority comes at a huge economic cost to the DPRK and they readily acknowledge this fact. One DPRK military officer has been quoted as saying that "no country will be able to maintain economic prosperity with a defense expenditure amounting to some 25 percent of the gross national product."[41] Pyongyang knows it must cut military spending if it is to promote economic growth.[42] But it will not cut military spending at the expense of its security. Thus, the true impetus for the DPRK to acquire nuclear weapons is an economic calculation. The ROK Ministry of Defense agrees that nuclear weapons development is an attempt by the DPRK to save its limited resources and assets while, at the same time, addressing its security concerns.[43] Nuclear weapons will allow it to reduce defense spending without sacrificing national security.

As it approaches the bilateral talks, the United States must understand that the DPRK regime is concerned primarily with its own survival. The DPRK has decided that nuclear weapons provide a certain level of security at a cheaper cost than the large conventional force that has to be maintained to counter the South's quality edge. Therefore, the United States must replace the gap in DPRK security that would have been filled with nuclear weapons if the DPRK is to give them up. Furthermore, any agreement on nuclear weapons must allow the DPRK to cut defense expenditures. From the DPRK perspective, not everything that the United States can offer in return is equivalent to the security of nuclear weapons and will also allow for decreased defense spending. For example, economic or trade concessions are probably poor substitutes for the type and amount of security assurance the DPRK desires. Such concessions would not allow the DPRK to decrease defense expenditures over the long term, as nuclear weapons would. That the 1994 Agreed Framework was centered around such guarantees probably says more about the effect of US military preparations on the non-nuclear DPRK psyche in 1993 and 1994 than the potential of buying the DPRK nuclear program in the future.[44] Beyond understanding the DPRK position, the United States must take steps to repair its alliance with the Republic of Korea (ROK) as it moves towards bilateral talks with the DPRK.

The alliance between the United States and the Republic of Korea has never been as solid or as well-defined as other alliances the United States has pursued. The alliance was initially born out of the Korean War, but not because Korea itself had intrinsic strategic importance. The alliance was first fostered because the implication of losing South Korea to the communist North and the impact this would have on other US allies was detrimental to US interests. Following the

Korean War and the advent of the Cold War, the ROK was important to the US policy of

containment. Following the end of the Cold War, the ROK has been seen as a stabilizing

country in Northeast Asia. So the ROK has only been important in the context of the overall US

strategy. As the interests of the United States have changed, so has the nature of the US-ROK

relationship. Unfortunately, for the leaders of the ROK, they can easily conclude that "the

meaning of South Korea to the United States can also be changed in the future."[45]

This evolution of the US-ROK alliance is important in understanding the ROK

perspective on the current nuclear crisis. Beyond the nuclear issue, the ROK, as evidenced by

several statements made by successive ROK presidents, "wants the United States to remain as a

regional power and as the single strongest military power in the region."[46] The ROK

understands they have always had second priority to overarching US interests and have

attempted to play their proper role. However, they also understand that any war will have far

greater negative effects on the ROK than the United States and that ROK security is more

directly threatened by the DPRK than US security. Unfortunately, as it stands now, the ROK has

"no means to extract guarantees about the US attitude to the security of South Korea."[47] But this

does not mean they will blindly accept any agreement unilaterally forged by the United States.

As ROK President Roh has stated, "Success or failure of a U.S. policy toward North Korea isn't

too big a deal to the American people, but it is a life-or-death matter for South Korea."[48] The

United States must restore the faith of the ROK government and their citizens in the commitment

of the United States to preserve and protect the Republic of Korea. To achieve this, to

paraphrase the Council of Foreign Relations Task Force on Korea, the US-ROK alliance must be

mended.[49] US efforts in this regard should focus on the ROK political leadership as well as the

ROK population because, in the end, both will have to enthusiastically support any bilateral agreement for it to succeed.

Much has been written about ROK public opinion attitudes towards the United States. Conventional wisdom places the ROK population in two camps, conservatives and progressives. "Generally, conservatives are described as staunchly pro-American while progressives are anti-American."[50] The conservatives are more likely to support a close partnership with the United States while the progressives see the United States, rather than the DPRK, as the primary cause of tension on the peninsula. These characterizations have a huge impact on the United States because the younger ROK generations tend to be more progressive than conservative.[51] It would be easy for the United States to dismiss any chance of winning over the ROK population to join in a united front against the DPRK in negotiations and to forge ahead on its own agenda in the bilateral talks.

However, there is hope that the United States can reconcile itself with the ROK citizens. A recent scientific polling study conducted by the Center for Strategic and International Studies offers a more nuanced view of the ROK population. The study concludes that progressives are still "wary of the United States…but nonetheless continue to value the U.S.-South Korean military alliance greatly."[52]

To simply label progressives as anti-American is misleading. Answers to specific survey questions show this to be true. In answering the survey, progressives agreed that the US alliance should be strengthened, US troops should not be withdrawn from the peninsula, and the ROK should not waver in its alliance with the United States.[53] Granted, there are significant ideological differences between conservatives and progressives but on the issue of the US-ROK alliance, both camps agree. So, in approaching the DPRK bilateral talks, the United States must build on this convergence of support within the ROK population. The divide between progressives and conservatives is not so large so as to prevent crafting a solution that is acceptable to both domestic camps. An agreement that is acceptable to the ROK population is eminently more desirable than one that is crafted without ROK input. In fact, it is probably mandatory for the long-term success of any agreement. Next, the United States must also improve its relationship with the ROK political leadership.

In the past, the United States has made unilateral decisions on issues of importance to the ROK such as US troop levels in Korea and negotiations strategy with the DPRK. Perhaps the United States felt it did not need to consult with Seoul prior to making any decisions or worse yet, maybe the United States felt that the ROK and its leaders had nothing useful to offer in the decision process. For example, President Bush called ROK President Kim Dae-jung "naïve" when Kim offered suggestions for engagement with the DPRK in 2001.[54]

Although the deterioration of the US-ROK alliance accelerated after the Cold War, it began to break down during President Carter's administration. In 1977, Carter announced that the United States would remove all US ground troops from South Korea.[55] To the chagrin of the ROK, he did not base this unilateral decision on common security factors, but rather the ROK human rights record and generally wanting to avoid another war in Asia.[56] During the early 1990s after the opening of the Berlin Wall, the alliance again was disrupted. In 1990, the United States announced it would withdraw 7000 personnel from the peninsula by 1992. It did so without consulting with the ROK on the decision or the impact of the withdrawal on the ROK security situation.[57] Shortly thereafter, President George H.W. Bush unilaterally decided to remove all nuclear weapons from the ROK.[58] During the George W. Bush administration, two more unilateral decisions were made that materially affected the ROK security environment.

15

First, in 2002, a decision was made to proceed with a hard line approach to negotiations with the DPRK, and then in 2004, another troop withdrawal was announced.[59]

This tendency for the United States to unilaterally make security decisions that affect the ROK is problematic for the relationship and must be avoided in the bilateral talks. As ROK President Roh said, in a veiled slight towards the United States, "People are often hurt when a close friend or partner appears to ignore their feelings or emotions."[60] Granted, some of those decisions were made with a larger strategic picture in mind, namely the Cold War. But from the ROK perspective, they were made to the detriment of its own security because they were not linked to any initiatives with the DPRK. As a ROK defense official wrote, "The ways of thinking and the methods that America used in making those [troop withdrawal and negotiation] decisions are not considered to be desirable ways to those concerned with the security of South Korea."[61] The United States and the ROK political leaders must have prior agreement on the strategy for bilateral talks because any solution that appears to sacrifice ROK security for US interests will ultimately fail. This is not an argument for trilateral talks, but rather a call for the United States to be aware of and supportive of ROK security concerns as it negotiates with the DPRK bilaterally. As it stands now in the Six Party Talks, "South Korea is the country that most consistently sides with the DPRK against the United States."[62] The United States must be sensitive to ROK concerns about their security and champion common goals at the negotiating table to mend their shaky alliance in the face of DPRK nuclear ambitions. The United States must understand that it is representing not only its own interests, but also those of the ROK when negotiating with the DPRK.

Conclusion

In conclusion, the end of the Cold War had profound implications for the situation on the Korean peninsula. Instead of lessening tension, the end of the Cold War increased the likelihood of a nuclear war on the Korean peninsula. The solution to this problem will not be simple or easy. Furthermore, the consequences of a military solution to the problem are nearly unthinkable. Sustained diplomatic efforts offer the best chance for a peaceful ending to the nuclear crisis but the prospect of success for the Six Party Talks is slim. The Six Party Talks are too slow and cumbersome due to how they are organized. Each country in the talks has a different reason for attending the talks and wanting a solution. This unnecessarily complicates the negotiations. Furthermore, the talks ultimately rely on China's influence over the DPRK for a negotiated solution but such faith in China's abilities may be misplaced.

For these reasons, the United States should abandon the Six Party Talks and engage in direct talks with the DPRK. Two operational themes must dominate this bilateral approach. First, the United States must understand that security is of utmost importance to the DPRK regime. The continued security of the DPRK must be considered as fundamental to any solution and, furthermore, any solution must allow the DPRK to reduce defense expenditures. Second, the United States must mend its alliance with the ROK with the understanding that ROK support is critical to a negotiated solution. ROK interests must be served if a diplomatic solution is to emerge and endure. The two most critical audiences in this effort are ROK leaders and the ROK population. Both are susceptible to true partnership efforts if US actions are seen to incorporate ROK concerns. In this partnership, the legacy of past US unilateral actions can be erased. A diplomatic solution must be found to the Korean nuclear crisis and bilateral talks centered on these ideas offer the best hope.

[1] Charles L. Pritchard, *Failed Diplomacy: The Tragic Story of How North Korea Got the Bomb* (Washington, DC: Brookings Institution Press, 2007), 132.

[2] Joel S. Wit, Daniel B. Poneman, and Robert L. Gallucci, *Going Critical: The First North Korean Nuclear Crisis* (Washington, DC: Brookings Institution Press, 2004), 5.

[3] For a comprehensive outline of the events leading up to the 1994 nuclear crisis and its ultimate settlement, see Chapter 10 in *Peace and Security in Northeast Asia: The Nuclear Issue and the Korean Peninsula*, edited by Young Whan Kihl and Peter Hayes.

[4] Brent Scowcroft and Arnold Kanter. "Korea: Time for Action." *The Washington Post*, 15 June 1994.

[5] In the major provision of the 1994 Agreed Framework, the United States agreed to provide heavy oil and light-water reactor (LWR) technology/equipment to the DPRK. In return, the DPRK agreed to cease construction of new reactors, stop the reprocessing of nuclear fuel, seal its nuclear laboratories, and place its facilities under IAEA inspection. For the full text of the 1994 Agreed Framework, see *Peace and Security in Northeast Asia: The Nuclear Issue and the Korean Peninsula*, edited by Young Whan Kihl and Peter Hayes.

[6] Young Whan Kihl and Peter Hayes, editors, *Peace and Security in Northeast Asia: The Nuclear Issue and the Korean Peninsula* (Armonk, NY: M.E. Sharpe Inc., 1997), 185.

[7] Pritchard, *Failed Diplomacy*, 44.

[8] Siegfried S. Hecker, "Denuclearizing North Korea," *Bulletin of the Atomic Scientists* 64, no. 2 (May/June 2008): 46.

[9] Ibid., 46.

[10] Ibid., 46. Note: To shut down a nuclear facility, the nuclear fuel must first be removed.

[11] Daniel J. Orcutt, *Carrot, Stick, or Sledgehammer: US Policy Options for North Korean Nuclear Weapons*, INSS Paper 56 (USAF Academy: Institute for National Security Studies, 2004), 44.

[12] For the identification and analysis of specific DPRK negotiating tactics, see *Negotiating with North Korea* by Richard Saccone.

[13] Susan Rosegrant, *Carrots, Sticks, and Question Marks: Negotiating the North Korean Nuclear Crisis,* Kennedy School of Government Case Program (Cambridge, MA: Kennedy School of Government, 1995).

[14] Victor D. Cha and David C. Kang, *Nuclear North Korea: A Debate on Engagement Strategies,* (New York, NY: Columbia University Press, 2003), 6.

[15] Wit, Poneman, and Gallucci, *Going Critical*, 104.

[16] Pritchard, *Failed Diplomacy*, 60.

[17] Ibid., 59.

[18] Yoichi Funabashi, *The Peninsula Question: A Chronicle of the Second Nuclear Crisis* (Washington, DC: Brookings Institution Press, 2007), 4.

[19] Pritchard, *Failed Diplomacy*, 97.

[20] Ibid., 96.

[21] Young Whan Kihl and Hong Nack Kim, editors, *North Korea: The Politics of Regime Survival* (Armonk, NY: M.E. Sharpe Inc., 2006), 259.

[22] Seung-Ho Joo and Tae-Hwan Kwak, editors, *North Korea's Second Nuclear Crisis and Northeast Asian Security* (Burlington, VT: Ashgate Publishing Company, 2007), 96.

[23] Information Office of the State Council of the People's Republic of China, "China's National Defense in 2002," *Xinhua News Agency*, 10 December 2002, http://news.xinhuanet.com/english/2002-12/10/content_654851.htm (accessed 10 January 2009).

[24] Gordon C. Chang, *Nuclear Showdown: North Korea Takes on the World* (New York, NY: Random House, 2006), 132.

[25] Pritchard, *Failed Diplomacy*, 60.

[26] Wit, Poneman, and Gallucci, *Going Critical*, 400.

[27] Bonnie S. Glaser and Wang Liang, "North Korea: The Beginning of a China-U.S. Partnership?," *The Washington Quarterly* 31, no.3 (Summer 2008):169

[28] Pritchard, *Failed Diplomacy*, 92.

[29] Joo and Kwak, *North Korea's Second Nuclear Crisis*, 109.

[30] Ahn Choong-yong, Nicholas Eberstadt, and Lee Young-sun, editors, *A New International Engagement Framework for North Korea? Contending Perspectives* (Washington, DC: Korea Economic Institute of America, 2004), 336.

[31] Joo and Kwak, *North Korea's Second Nuclear Crisis*, 107.

[32] Terence Roehrig, *From Deterrence to Engagement: The U.S. Defense Commitment to South Korea* (Lanham, MD: Lexington Books, 2006), 221.

[33] Ibid., 221.

[34] Han S. Park, editor, *North Korea: Ideology, Politics, Economy* (Englewood Cliffs, NJ: Prentice-Hall, Inc., 1996), 222.

[35] Ibid., 11.

[36] Ibid., 223.

[37] Pritchard, *Failed Diplomacy*, 19.

[38] Roehrig, *From Deterrence to Engagement*, 98.

[39] Park, *North Korea*, 207.

[40] Roehrig, *From Deterrence to Engagement*, 82.

[41] Park, *North Korea*, 226.

[42] Ibid., 226.

[43] Roehrig, *From Deterrence to Engagement*, 97.

[44] For a narrative of the extensive US military preparations during the 1994 nuclear crisis, see pages 204-220 of Wit, Poneman, and Galluci's book *Going Critical*.

[45] Kim Jung-Ik, *The Future of the US-Republic of Korea Military Relationship* (New York, NY: St. Martin's Press, 1996), 30.

[46] Ibid., 118.

[47] Ibid., 157.

[48] Chang, *Nuclear Showdown*, 112.

[49] Council on Foreign Relations, *Meeting the North Korean Nuclear Challenge* (New York, NY: Council on Foreign Relations, 2003), 36.

[50] Haesook Chae and Steven Kim, "Conservatives and Progressives in South Korea," *The Washington Quarterly* 31, no.4 (Autumn 2008): 84.

[51] Ibid., 78-79.

[52] Ibid., 78.

[53] Ibid., 86.

[54] Pritchard, *Failed Diplomacy*, 52.

[55] This decision was never implemented due to new intelligence that indicated the size of the DPRK's conventional military was 80 percent larger than previously estimated.

[56] Roehrig, *From Deterrence to Engagement*, 135.

[57] Jung-Ik, *Future of the US-Republic of Korea Military Relationship*, 112.

[58] Ibid., 122.

[59] Roehrig, *From Deterrence to Engagement*, 145, 163, & 223.

[60] Chang, *Nuclear Showdown*, 113.

[61] Jung-Ik, *Future of the US-Republic of Korea Military Relationship*, 123-124.

[62] Chang, *Nuclear Showdown*, 112.

Bibliography

Albright, David, and Kevin O'Neill, eds. *Solving the North Korean Nuclear Puzzle*. Washington, DC: Institute for Science and International Security Press, 2000.

Bermudez Jr., Joseph S. *The Armed Forces of North Korea*. New York, NY: I.B. Tauris & Co., 2001.

Cha, Victor D., and David C. Kang. *Nuclear North Korea*: *A Debate on Engagement Strategies*. New York, NY: Columbia University Press, 2003.

Chae, Haesook, and Steven Kim. "Conservatives and Progressives in South Korea." *The Washington Quarterly* 31:4 (Autumn 2008): 77-95.

Chang, Gordon G. *Nuclear Showdown: North Korea Takes on the World*. New York, NY: Random House, 2006.

Choong-yong, Ahn, Nicholas Eberstadt, and Lee Young-sun. *A New International Engagement Framework for North Korea?: Contending Perspectives*. Washington, DC: Korea Economic Institute of America, 2004.

Council on Foreign Relations. *Meeting the North Korean Nuclear Challenge*. New York, NY: Council on Foreign Relations, 2003.

Dong, Wonmo, ed. *The Two Koreas and the United States*. Armonk, NY: M.E. Sharpe, 2000.

Ford, Glyn, and Soyoung Kwon. *North Korea on the Brink: Struggle for Survival*. Ann Arbor, MI: Pluto Press, 2008.

Funabashi, Yoichi. *The Peninsula Question: A Chronicle of the Second Korean Nuclear Crisis*. Washington, DC: Brookings Institution Press, 2007.

Glaser, Bonnie S. and Wang Liang. "North Korea: The Beginning of a China-U.S. Partnership?" *The Washington Quarterly* 31, no. 3 (Summer 2008): 165-180.

Hecker, Siegfried S. "Denuclearizing North Korea." *Bulletin of the Atomic Scientists* 64, no. 10 (May/June 2008): 44-49, 61-62.

Hunter, Helen-Louise. *Kim Il-Song's North Korea*. Westport, CT: Praeger Publishers, 1999.

Information Office of the State Council of the People's Republic of China. "China's National Defense in 2002." *Xinhua News Agency*, 10 December 2002. http://news.xinhuanet.com/english/2002-12/10/content_654851.htm (accessed 10 January 2009)

Joo, Seung-Ho and Tae-Hwan Kwak, eds. *North Korea's Second Nuclear Crisis and Northeast Asian Security*. Burlington, VT: Ashgate Publishing Co., 2007.

Jung-Ik, Kim. *The Future of the US-Republic of Korea Military Relationship.* New York, NY: St. Martin's Press, 1996.

Kerchner, Colonel Scott E. "The Six-Party Talks: The Right Solution to the Democratic People's Republic of Korea Nuclear Weapons Program." Master's thesis, US Army War College, 2005.

Kihl, Young Whan, and Peter Hayes, eds. *Peace and Security in Northeast Asia: The Nuclear Issue and the Korean Peninsula.* Armonk, NY: M.E. Sharpe, 1997.

Kihl, Young Whan, and Hong Nack Kim, eds. *North Korea: The Politics of Regime Survival.* Armonk, NY: M.E. Sharpe, 2006.

Orcutt, Daniel. *Carrot, Stick, or Sledgehammer: US Policy Options for North Korean Nuclear Weapons.* INSS Paper 56. USAF Academy: Institute for National Security Studies, 2004.

Park, Han S., ed. *North Korea: Ideology, Politics, Economy.* Englewood Cliffs, NJ: Prentice-Hall Inc., 1996.

Pritchard, Charles L. *Failed Diplomacy: The Tragic Story of How North Korea Got the Bomb.* Washington, DC: Brookings Institution Press, 2007.

Roehrig, Terence. *From Deterrence to Engagement: The U.S. Defense Commitment to South Korea.* Lanham, MD: Lexington Books, 2006.

Rosegrant, Susan. *Carrots, Sticks, and Question Marks: Negotiating the North Korean Nuclear Crisis.* Kennedy School of Government Case Program. Cambridge, MA: Kennedy School of Government, 1995.

Saccone, Richard. *Negotiating with North Korea.* Elizabeth, NJ: Hollym International Corporation, 2003.

Scobell, Andrew. *Projecting Pyongyang: The Future of North Korea's Kim Jong Il Regime.* Carlisle, PA: Strategic Studies Institute, 2008.

Scowcroft, Brent, and Arnold Kanter. "Korea: Time for Action." *The Washington Post*, 15 June 1994.

Sigal, Leon V. *Disarming Strangers: Nuclear Diplomacy with North Korea.* Princeton, NJ: Princeton University Press, 1998.

Wit, Joel S., Daniel B. Poneman, and Robert L. Galluci. *Going Critical: The First North Korean Nuclear Crisis.* Washington, DC: Brookings Institution Press, 2004.

Xinbo, Wu. "A Forward-Looking Partner in a Changing East Asia." *The Washington Quarterly* 31:4 (Autumn 2008): 155-163.